THE TRIPOLITAN WAR, 1801–1805

Shortly after gaining its independence from England, the United States chose to fight the pirates of Barbary rather than pay them tribute, as did all other nations that traded in the Mediterranean Sea. The decision was bold, its conclusion long delayed, but the eventual victory by the tiny United States Navy broke a pattern of international blackmail dating back more than one hundred and fifty years.

PRINCIPALS

THOMAS JEFFERSON, third U.S. President, who thought tribute to Barbary "a degrading yoke."

STEPHEN DECATUR, a U.S. naval hero for all seasons.

WILLIAM EATON, who led the U.S. Marines "to the shores of Tripoli."

EDWARD PREBLE, a senior U.S. naval officer who inspired young men.

WILLIAM BAINBRIDGE, a U.S. Navy captain hounded by misfortune.

JAMES CATHCART, a U.S. consul who had been a pirate's slave.

YUSUF, pasha of Tripoli, a murderer and usurper.

HAMET, Yusuf's brother, friend of William Eaton.

TWO DEYS OF ALGIERS, "a huge, shaggy beast" and "a ferocious old man."

"Burning of the Frigate Philadelphia *in the Harbor of Tripoli." A painting by Edward Moran in the U.S. Naval Academy Museum. (U.S. Naval Academy Museum from Cushing)*

A FOCUS BOOK

The Tripolitan War, 1801-1805

America Meets the Menace of the Barbary Pirates

by Henry Castor

Illustrated with contemporary prints

FRANKLIN WATTS, INC.
845 Third Avenue, New York, N.Y. 10022

The authors and publishers of the Focus Books wish to acknowledge the helpful editorial suggestions of Professor Richard B. Morris.

Contents

THE TRIPOLITAN WAR, 1801–1805

A pirate ship of the Barbary Coast. Lateen-rigged, with sleek hull lines, these ships were extremely fast and thus made excellent buccaneering vessels. (Charles Phelps Cushing)

When the Mediterranean Was a "Pirate Lake"

About on a line with San Francisco or Washington, D.C., along the north coast of Africa, lie the white, sunbaked cities of Tangier, Algiers, and Tunis. Three hundred miles south-southeast of Tunis stands Tripoli. All of these cities are seaports, and in bygone times were known as Barbary.

The word "Barbary" recalls the Berbers, one of the many races or nations which have swept over this land of long and stormy history. The scene today looks much as it did when President Thomas Jefferson ordered warships there to punish the pirates of Tripoli. Indeed, it has changed little from the time of the Carthaginians, rivals of ancient Rome, traces of whose dead city lie outside modern Tunis.

The shoreline at Tangier, Morocco, opposite the Rock of Gibraltar, is itself rocky, and so continues eastward to Cape Bon in Tunisia. There it veers sharply to the south and becomes low, shoaling, and reef-bound along the Libyan and Egyptian shores to the mouths of the Nile. The land is hot and dry, its settled population clustered about coastal water holes, while the nomadic Arabs of the interior drift among Saharan oases. North-

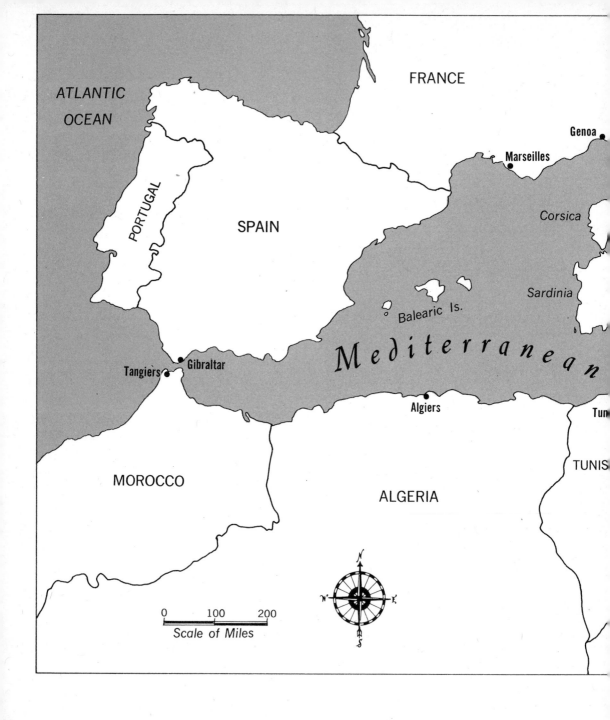

erly gales lash the coasts in winter, now as ever threatening to break the keels of ships on Barbary's rocks and reefs.

Although the gales persist, the pirates are gone. The tradition of the Mediterranean being known as a pirate lake was even more ancient than Carthage, for no less a personage than Theseus, legendary king of Athens, enjoyed piracy as a kind of gentlemanly summer sport. However, the professional pirates of Barbary date from the Turkish conquest of 1518, when Khayr al-Din, also called Redbeard, established his lair at Algiers. Technically, the sea robbers were "corsairs," meaning seamen who were granted licenses by a government to steal. In Europe and America corsairs were called privateers.

Besides the prospect of plunder, piracy also provided an outlet for religious hostility. During the era of the war galley, the oars of Muslim boats usually were stroked by Christian slaves, while those of European galleys might be manned by Muslims, although ordinarily their rowers were homebred criminals and heretics.

Among the famous prisoners ransomed from the shackles of a galley bench were Vincent de Paul, sainted for his charities; François Arago, the astronomer who measured the planets; and Miguel de Cervantes, author of *Don Quixote*. James Cathcart and Richard O'Brien, who later were United States consuls in Barbary, were captives in Algiers, where the enterprising Cathcart made a tidy fortune by running a chain of slave-operated taverns and became secretary to the dey.

Punitive expeditions launched against the corsairs failed to root them out, although all the powers of Europe took at least

[6]

Khayr al-Din, better known as "Red-beard," was one of the most famous of the early Barbary corsairs. He died in the year 1546. (Charles Phelps Cushing)

one turn from the sixteenth century onward. Before the Americans became involved, the last full-dress assault was led by a Spanish count named O'Reilly, in 1775.

The sea rovers sometimes were joined by European renegades who adopted the religion of Islam as the key to fortune and taught their hosts new skills in navigation and shipbuilding. One was a Scot named Peter Lisle, alias Murad Rais, who married a daughter of the pasha of Tripoli and commanded his fleet against the Americans.

Common piracy blossomed into a sophisticated racket in 1662, when England revived the ancient custom of paying tribute. The corsairs agreed to spare English ships for an annual

[7]

bribe paid in gold, jewels, arms, or supplies, as the pirates wished. The custom spread to all countries trading in the Mediterranean, large or small, and was not completely blotted out until the French began to occupy North Africa in 1830.

With its mighty sea power, Great Britain could easily have exterminated the nests of the corsairs. However, the advisers of Charles II chose to buy peace for the shameless reason that allowing piracy to continue acted as a damper on England's seagoing merchant competitors. As Benjamin Franklin put it, "[There is] a maxim among merchants, that if there were no Algiers, it would be worth England's while to build one."

The pirate lords learned to be wary about honoring too many hands-off treaties at any one time, for they always needed two or three victims for their cutthroats to attack. Barbary's rulers seldom died in bed unless by poison; by keeping his subjects' scimitars busy on the infidels at sea, a ruler reduced the possibility that they would turn them on himself.

England paid tribute for the vessels of her American colonies, and France guaranteed it for them during the War of Independence. The new United States awoke abruptly to an ugly responsibility of independence when in 1785 the dey of Algiers seized an American ship and jailed its crew for ransom.

Yet the cunning dey was in no hurry to wring tribute from his new source of revenue. For awhile, at least, the capture of ships would be more profitable, and in view of the naval weakness of the United States, would be entirely safe. So eleven of the first unfortunate Americans to fall into his hands died before their country ransomed the rest ten years later.

Tribute from "Fat Ducks"

Merchant ships flying a unique starred and striped flag became more and more visible on the high seas after 1783. By the turn of the century, eighty American vessels were regularly calling at Mediterranean ports.

In the eyes of the sea hawks of Barbary, they were "fat ducks," a view actively encouraged by Britain and France. The upstart traders of the New World could stand a bit of thinning out by the corsairs. As one English official said, "That the Barbary States are advantageous to the [existing] maritime powers is obvious. . . . The Americans cannot protect themselves [since] they cannot pretend to a navy."

Turkey, overlord of Barbary, was an ally of England. Barbary needed free trade with France. Hence the pirates were forbidden to attack British shipping and in plain self-interest could not raid the French. With his targets so limited, the dey of Algiers found the American fat ducks to be godsends. By 1794 this "ferocious old man," as James Cathcart knew him, had plundered eleven American ships, and held one hundred and nineteen of their survivors for ransom.

[9]

President George Washington tried to reach an understanding with the Barbary States with little success. His agents, one of whom was John Paul Jones, the naval hero of 1779, either died before achieving anything or had doors slammed in their faces. Only Thomas Barclay won a point in Tangier, when in 1787 he persuaded the sultan of Morocco to sign a peace treaty to run for fifty years and paid only a token gift to bind it.

America's ambassadors in Europe worked to free Americans enslaved in Algerian dungeons, but the agents of Benjamin Franklin, John Adams, and Thomas Jefferson were cold-shouldered by the dey. When the Barbary ruler did condescend to talk, his demands outraged one ambassador. Mr. Jefferson declared that tribute was "money thrown away," and that the most convincing argument that could be used on pirates was gunpowder and shot.

But the next President, John Adams, insisted on paying for peace as did the rest of the civilized world. Congress agreed, and in 1795 it authorized payment of tribute. Algiers was granted the equivalent of $642,500 in cash, munitions, and a 36-gun frigate, besides a yearly tribute of $21,600 worth of naval supplies. So at long last, scores of American captives again walked into the light, except for thirty-seven dead, whose ransoms had to be paid nevertheless.

News of the rich windfall prompted Tunis and Tripoli to demand and to be promised their own blood money, scaled down to their lesser nuisance value. The Algerian settlement would brew envy in Tripoli; on second thought the pasha suspected that he had accepted too little too soon.

[10]

James Cathcart, the former slave of the dey of Algiers, was appointed consul to Tripoli in 1799. His impression of the character of the lords of Barbary was not one of awe. On the contrary, Cathcart suggested that American tribute should be delivered by warships with their guns run out, a display which would "work on the rulers like electricity."

William Eaton, consul at Tunis, was even more positive about the benefits of firmness. There could be "no permanent friendship with [the pirates] without paving the way with gold or cannonballs, and the proper question is which method is preferable." He answered his own question pungently. "Congress should check the insolence of these scoundrels . . . [or] wrest the quiver of arrows from the left talon of the eagle . . . and substitute a fiddle bow or a segar."

William Eaton, a major figure in the Barbary wars, was a graduate of Dartmouth College, and served as a U.S. Army captain until 1798. He was sent to Tunis in that year as American consul. It was Eaton who, in 1805, would lead the famous march to capture the city of Derna in the United States efforts to subdue the Tripolitan pirate state. (Charles Phelps Cushing)

However, calls to boldness were unheard in Congress. Indeed, the legislators even considered asking little Portugal if its warships would convoy American shipping — for a reasonable fee, of course.

A Voyage to Turkey

An absurd episode in 1800 pointed up the feebleness of American response to corsair arrogance. When the frigate *George Washington* docked at Algiers with a consignment of tribute, a brilliant idea struck the dey. To impress his master, the sultan of Turkey, with his power and importance, he would commandeer the American ship to run an errand for him.

Captain William Bainbridge therefore was instructed to haul down the American flag and to run up the Algerian colors. Besides taking on a million dollars in treasure, the captain was made responsible for safe passage of the Algerian ambassador to Turkey, his retinue of one hundred, a like number of slaves, and a deckload of livestock which included a few lions. The black mouths of cannon ringing the pirate harbor suggested to Captain Bainbridge that he had better swallow the insult and obey.

The voyage to Constantinople was smelly, cramped, and noisy, with some of the passengers roaring their unhappiness. The crew tripped over prostrate Muslims who swarmed on deck five times daily to bow toward Mecca in prayer, and some of

Captain William Bainbridge, an American naval officer often hounded by misfortune. (Charles Phelps Cushing)

the faithful nursed suspicions of the Americans sailing the ark. Not all Algerians were seamen; those with no knowledge of tacking a ship into the wind thought the infidels were deliberately trying to confuse them about the direction of Mecca.

Bainbridge protested to the sultan of Turkey and was assured that no other American ship would ever have to suffer the indignity his had. But American prestige in the Mediterranean plunged to zero. Being respecters of brute force only, the corsairs of Barbary now were certain that the United States of America was the poorest-spirited nation on earth, not excluding the kingdom of Naples.

[14]

The Birth of a Navy

In the spring of 1785 the last warship of the old Continental Congress was sold to be converted for commercial use, and for twelve years thereafter no American navy existed. There was a time also when the entire regular army of the United States could have been barracked in one roomy Pennsylvania Dutch barn. It mustered just eighty-three men and a captain.

This was the "critical period" of American history, when the raw young nation was deep in debt, economically shaken, unsure of itself, and in danger of becoming embroiled in Europe's power struggle. Yet the weakness of its government under the Articles of Confederation does not explain the widespread prejudice against a national military establishment. Rather, it was the hatred of conscription, of uniforms, and of standing armies that was ingrained in the American soul.

As for a war fleet, said the rising Democratic Republicans, this would be "but the entering wedge of a new monarchy in America." Let the militia and privateer navies of the various states shield the Republic!

Yet in the very year that the United States stripped itself

of its last fighting ship, the corsairs of Barbary began to rob its merchantmen. The simple reason why no American diplomat could command attention in Barbary was that he and everyone else knew that no naval fist could be clenched to back up his words.

If piracy was a serious nuisance, estrangement from France split the United States asunder and threatened disaster. Relations between the two former allies indeed did crumble into a real, though undeclared, naval war from 1798 to 1800.

Tensions with France and England, and the mounting clamor of merchants for protection against the corsairs, compelled Congress to vote money for warships in 1794, but with something short of wild enthusiasm. John Adams' Federalists, many of them New Englanders dependent on foreign trade, voted aye, but Thomas Jefferson's Republicans stuck stubbornly to the view that a national navy was a blow to states' freedom.

In July, 1797, at a Philadelphia shipyard where a teen-aged Stephen Decatur was working, the frigate *United States* slid into the Schuylkill with such hurrah that she bumped the opposite bank of the river. Soon she was joined by *Constitution* out of Boston and *Constellation* out of Baltimore. These beautiful ships were designed by naval architect Joshua Humphreys, a Philadelphia Quaker, and would score a record of victory at sea unmatched in their time.

Triumph was built into them. Humphreys planned his ships to be "superior to any European frigate . . . and never [to be] obliged to go into action but on their own terms." This

The U.S.S. Constellation, *one of the famous frigates designed by Joshua Humphreys. (Charles Phelps Cushing)*

meant that they outgunned their own class but could still outrun larger ships.

Humphreys' scrutiny of details was total; he even selected the timber used, from false keel to main truck. New England cedar planking braced by Georgia live-oak frames created vessels so solid that when some cannonballs bounced off *Constitution* in her first engagement, she became forever known as Old Ironsides. The U.S.S. *Constitution* and *Constellation* are still listed as active vessels of the United States Navy.

The purchased peace with Algiers caused the conservative gentlemen of Congress to cancel shipbuilding, but the hostile revolutionary French Directory, by its contemptuous seizures of merchantmen, pushed Congress to reconsider and to declare reprisals in 1798. An independent Navy Department was begun under the efficient Benjamin Stoddert of Maryland, and more superfrigates were laid down, among them *Philadelphia*, gift of the nation's capital to the nation. After the "quasi war" with France, Congress again decided to cut back frigate strength, now down to thirteen, only six of which might sail on duty at a time.

Even reckoned in dollars, the decision was a blunder, for the entire cost of a vigorous naval program would have been far less than the value of ships lost to African corsairs and European privateers. Yet cost and savings were irrelevant to Republican thinking; they simply believed that a high-seas navy menaced peace abroad and democracy at home. Indeed, it is an ironical joke of history that pro-navy John Adams preferred to pay

[18]

tribute, while anti-navy Thomas Jefferson would fight rather than be blackmailed.

The warships were few and poorly supplied — their crews often went hungry and half-naked — and mustered almost as many foreigners as native Americans. But no longer could a European coolly say, "The United States cannot pretend to a navy." For as the undeclared naval war with France had shown, the United States Navy had commanded much respect for the new flag at sea. In their duels with ships of the French Directory, American captains lost only once. In that instance the 14-gun sloop *Retaliation* was captured by a ruse by two frigates mounting eighty cannon.

The master of *Retaliation* was rarely lucky. His name was William Bainbridge.

Yusuf Chops Down a Flagpole

His Highness, Yusuf, pasha of Tripoli, overlooked no crime or misdemeanor that might serve his personal greed or ambition. In fact, he had gained his throne by murdering his oldest brother before the very eyes of their mother.

Yusuf's style ran to swagger as well as to murder. Among the trifles he had ordered for himself as part of the American tribute were several diamond-studded guns. But he outdid him-. self for gall on the occasion of the death of George Washington. The pasha informed President Adams that it was customary when a great man passed on for a tributary state to make a gift in his name to the crown of Tripoli. Yusuf estimated Washington's worth at about $10,000.

His impatience with America grew, not without cause from his point of view, since by the spring of 1801 he had not seen one cent of the loot promised five years before. At last he summoned James Cathcart to kiss his plump hand and to hear his decree that, as a penalty, tribute would be raised to $225,000, plus $25,000 annually in goods of his (Yusuf's) choice. If re-fused, the alternative was war.

Cathcart dispatched the pasha's message to President Jefferson, but he anticipated the President's answer by leaving for Italy. On May 14 a party of soldiers chopped down the flagpole in front of the American consulate, a significant gesture in a land of no tall trees — and one that meant war.

Thomas Jefferson would not hear of this curious ceremony for weeks, but coincidentally on May 20 he ordered a ceremony of his own: "showing the flag," as a visit by warships to foreign waters was called. The new President had been appalled to discover that tribute and ransoms paid to Barbary had exceeded $2,000,000, or about one-fifth of the entire annual income of the United States government.

Since America had a navy, the anti-navy President decided to put it to work. When Captain Richard Dale dropped anchor at Gibraltar in early summer of 1801 he was commodore (the courtesy title of a squadron leader) of the frigates *President*, *Essex*, and *Philadelphia*, and the sloop *Enterprise*. He quickly struck a bargain with the Swedish naval commander in the area to help blockade Tripoli and convoy American shipping, since Sweden too was quarreling with Tripoli at the time.

But even with Swedish help, Dale's mission proved to be impossible. Pirate cruisers at Gibraltar under Murad Rais, Yusuf's Scottish son-in-law, required watching. This forced the weak American expedition to try to cover both Tripoli and Gibraltar, which were 1,200 miles apart, resulting in "a most desultory blockade." Dale's supply system broke down, his men were chronically hungry, and many died of scurvy.

The lone success of the squadron was the defeat of a larger

[21]

Captain Richard Dale, leader of the American naval squadron to Tripoli in 1801. (U.S. Naval Academy from Cushing)

Tripolitan ship by *Enterprise*. Since there had been no declaration of war by the United States, Lieutenant Andrew Sterrett could not take the cruiser as a prize. However, he did heave all of its guns overboard before allowing the ship to continue on its way, with sixty casualties to his none.

Yusuf was so furious at his captain's defeat that he had him *bastinadoed* (beaten on the soles of his feet) and paraded backward on a donkey, his neck festooned with sheep's entrails.

At this time, U.S. naval enlistments were for one year only, so in March, 1802, Commodore Dale sailed home with sailors whose service was over. Congress still refused to declare the unpleasantness with Tripoli a war, but did levy a light war tax and proclaimed "protection of commerce" by the navy. When Sweden settled her differences with the pirates, the tiny United States Navy had to police the Mediterranean alone.

Commodore Dale was replaced by the faltering and sickly Commodore Richard Morris, whose squadron straggled haphazardly across the Atlantic. Once it had arrived on station, Morris and his "commanding" wife became ornaments of the social whirl of the British garrisons at Gibraltar and Malta, which left the commodore too exhausted to get on with the war. Storms, breakdowns, and desertions plagued the American ships, but above all Morris's incompetence aborted the few ragged attacks he attempted. His laxness infected his officers; the pugnacious William Eaton said that more Yankee blood was being shed by dueling in the park than in battle.

The unhappy U.S. consul at Tunis scorned the do-nothing navy. Besides, William Eaton was a former Indian fighter, and he was unhappy in a country whose greatest virtue (he said) was "the absence of lawyers . . . [but it is] infested with priests."

Eaton despised Barbary's vermin, filth, and corruption, and he especially resented having to remove his shoes and bow to kiss the perfumed hands of princely thieves and murderers. Most of all, he seethed over the indignities heaped upon him as the representative of poor-spirited America; he said he could not talk with a Tunisian official "without exciting a grimace of contempt and ridicule."

If reduced to it, Eaton declared that he would even serve in Siberia, but "Barbary is hell."

Eaton's woes multiplied when his own shipping ventures

[23]

fell on bad times. Among his other debts, he had borrowed heavily to ransom an Italian countess from a Turkish harem. When Commodore Morris went ashore to confer with Eaton in February, that officer was stunned at being jailed by the bey as security for the consul's debts.

Morris managed to find part of the sum and was freed a month later, but the countess's family never did repay the gallant Eaton. In June the bumbling commodore and generous consul both sailed home. The sorry Morris would be dismissed from the navy and forgotten. Eaton would gain the ear and confidence of James Madison, secretary of state, and return to brief glory in Tripoli.

The man who succeeded Morris as commodore in September of 1803, Captain Edward Preble, shared his predecessor's inclination toward bad health. Aside from that, their characters were as different as day from night.

"The Most Bold and Daring
Act of the Age"

The fine new frigate *Philadelphia* arrived in the Mediterranean ahead of Commodore Preble's squadron and somewhat unwisely set about trying to blockade Tripoli all alone. On October 31, while pursuing a corsair under full sail, *Philadelphia* grounded on a sandbar about two miles offshore. Despite five hours of desperate work by her crew, she stuck fast. With her broadsides tilted at crazy angles, her firing was harmless to the pirates' small craft that quickly swarmed about her.

After jettisoning his useless cannon, and thinking the ship's carpenter had scuttled the ship, *Philadelphia*'s captain surrendered to prevent a massacre. Among the three hundred and seven Americans taken prisoner were young David Porter and Jacob Jones, both of whom were just beginning brilliant naval careers.

After the war, a court of inquiry decided that the captain of *Philadelphia* had "acted with fortitude," and so cleared his name, but clouds of suspicion always seemed to hang over the unlucky William Bainbridge.

News of this disaster, wrote Commodore Preble, "dis-

Captain Edward Preble, the much-respected senior naval officer who became commodore of the Tripoli squadron in 1803. Preble had a gift for inspiring young officers serving under him, many of whom later went on to brilliant naval careers. (Charles Phelps Cushing)

tresses me beyond description," and it served to offset the effect of his strategic victory at Tangier a few weeks earlier. At that time, the sultan of Morocco had been complaining that the treaty of 1787 was worthless to him, while Algiers was fattening on American tribute. Preble determined to have a word with him on his way to Tripoli; in the harbor of Tangier he opened *Constitution*'s gunports and ran out her cannon to frighten the inhabitants of the city. Then Preble went ashore to call on the sultan.

Whether it was the American officer's stern, cool warning that influenced the sultan, or the threat of broadsides aimed at

[26]

his palace, the Moroccan ruler hastened to agree that his father's treaty was so good that it must last forever. In token of his sincerity, the sultan presented the commodore with some fresh meat.

Thus, Morocco was pacified for the moment, but Preble heard that the bey of Tunis was also showing belligerence, made bold by American fumbling against Tripoli. Clearly some decisive action was overdue. Yet the commodore hesitated to begin bombarding the city, for this would result in the bey's murdering *Philadelphia*'s helpless crewmen in reprisal. So, as agent for Consul General Tobias Lear, the new negotiator he had brought with him from Washington, Preble first offered $50,000 and then $100,000 for their release, but was scornfully refused. Whereupon, young Stephen Decatur was ordered to set a plan of his in motion.

In December, Lieutenant Decatur in "lucky little *Enterprise*" had apprehended an enemy ketch, a four-gun vessel of shallow draft which could be rowed. Meanwhile, the Danish consul, Nicholas Nissen, had been exchanging letters written in invisible ink between Preble and Captain Bainbridge. The worried captive reported that the pirates had refloated *Philadelphia*, fished up her guns, and were rigging her for action against her sister ships. Decatur's plan for a raid to destroy the unlucky frigate called for the use of a native vessel, and the captured ketch filled the bill.

The raiders sailed from Malta, arriving off Tripoli on the night of February 15, 1804. Trailing *Intrepid*, the former Tripolitan *Mastico*, came the new brig *Siren*, Lieutenant Charles

[27]

A portrait of Stephen Decatur, later in his career. As a lieutenant serving under Preble, he carried out the daring mission of destroying the U.S. frigate Philadelphia, *then held by the Barbary pirates. (Charles Phelps Cushing)*

Stewart commanding, whose job was to pick up survivors of the raid, if any. The sailors dimly visible on *Intrepid*'s deck wore Maltese dress, and a few Maltese were among the eighty-four volunteers aboard. Among those crouched out of sight were young James Lawrence and an even younger Thomas Macdonough, both of whom were later to write their names large in American naval history.

The Maltese pilot of *Intrepid* hailed the big frigate; he had lost his anchor and could he tie up to *Philadelphia* for the night? If the pirates had taken the slightest alarm over the tiny craft drifting toward them, one massive broadside from the frigate could have completely disintegrated her.

But all was calm until the ships bumped. Then, as a pirate reported later, the Americans "sent a Decatur on a dark night, with a band of Christian dogs fierce and cruel as the tiger, who killed our brothers and burnt our ships before our eyes."

Decatur's boarding party flung grappling hooks to lash the rails together, and yelling and screaming, leaped onto the deck of the frigate. Some of them wielded tomahawks, killing twenty pirates in as many minutes and chasing the rest over the side. Only one raider was wounded before *Philadelphia* was set afire in four places. Then the Americans withdrew.

Decatur's amazing luck held good in the even more perilous escape from the harbor. Artillery thundered wildly from out of the night, including the flame-touched guns of *Philadelphia*, but the little ketch, scarcely scratched, was rowed away to rejoin *Siren*.

When Admiral Lord Nelson heard of the raid, he called it

In this historical painting, Lieutenant Decatur leads his boarding party aboard the Philadelphia. *(Charles Phelps Cushing)*

"the most bold and daring act of the age." Coming from the first naval genius of the times, who would die at Trafalgar the following year, this was praise indeed. Stephen Decatur, just turned twenty-five, won promotion to captain — then the highest rank in the navy — and he remains the youngest man ever to be so honored.

Decatur's act, no matter how bold and daring, nevertheless was flawed. True, a menace had been wiped out, but she had been an American ship to begin with. And to salt the irony, the first captain of Philadelphia-built, Philadelphia-donated *Philadelphia* had been Commodore Stephen Decatur of Philadelphia, father of the young Philadelphian who put her to the torch.

The Philadelphia *blazes fore and aft in Tripoli harbor. (Charles Phelps Cushing)*

"Preble's Boys" at Tripoli

Tripoli was defended by 25,000 soldiers and 115 cannon ashore, with 24 warships guarding the harbor. Against them Commodore Preble could pit only 1,060 men aboard 7 ships, of which only *Constitution* was heavy-gunned.

To add a bit more firepower to his small fleet, the commodore hired eight gunboats from the king of Naples. These were shallow-water craft, each mounting one large cannon or mortar, and they could be rowed. If he could not force the pasha to surrender, Preble said, at least he had "seven hundred bombshells and plenty of shot to amuse him with."

Armed American boarding parties went aboard the gunboats under the command of Decatur, and Lieutenant Richard Somers, an old school friend of Decatur's. The ninety-six Neapolitan sailors working the boats were not expected to join in any boarding action.

On August 3, Commodore Preble's squadron sailed in to open a two-hour bombardment of the city of Tripoli. But the pirates were sheltered safe behind thick-walled defenses, one of which, "Fort America," had been built by *Philadelphia's*

Detail of a large painting in the U.S. Naval Academy Museum shows the Battle of Tripoli in full swing. Note a portion of Preble's hired gunboats at right, being rowed. Frigate Constitution *is out of picture at far right. (U.S. Naval Academy Museum from Cushing)*

Heavily wounded in the naval engagement at Tripoli was Lieutenant John Trippe. (U.S. Naval Academy Museum from Cushing)

crew under the lash. They had also been forced into carrying ammunition for the corsair artillery during the bombardment. By his persistent bad luck, William Bainbridge was injured when a wall collapsed on him.

When Preble finally disengaged and put out to sea, the only satisfaction he could draw from his attack was the success of his gunboats. Preble's bombardment of Tripoli had caused little damage, but the behavior of Decatur's outnumbered crews pleased the commodore — all the more because the hard-bitten pirates were supposed to be invincible at hand-to-hand fighting. But never again would they attempt their favorite method of attacking, boarding, upon an American ship. American sailors led by men like Lieutenant John Trippe, outnumbered three to one, still killed twenty-one of the corsairs and captured fifteen in one engagement alone. Trippe himself took eleven wounds from a Turkish captain before ending the combat with a pike thrust. Three Tripolitan gunboats were captured, and one sunk.

Only one American was lost; Decatur's younger brother, James, had been treacherously shot by the captain of a pirate ship after its surrender. Stephen avenged the boy by killing his murderer in a savage man-to-man encounter before witnesses.

Preble returned to shell the enemy five more times, but without troops to storm the forts, the effect was slight. His frustration was made complete on August 7 when the frigate *John Adams* arrived with news that four more frigates were following, one of them bearing a replacement for the commodore. To the chagrin of Thomas Jefferson, who greatly admired Preble, the fighting commodore had fallen victim to red tape involving seniority.

Preble admitted that his feelings were "lacerated by this supersedure," but his officers, none of them over thirty, would never forget "the Old Man." (The tall, slim Preble was only forty-two himself.) The younger men had begun by resenting his iron-handed discipline, but most would live to be proud of the name "Preble's Boys." A sketch of their exploits in the War of 1812 appears in the *Appendix* of this book.

Two young officers who did not survive were Richard Somers and Henry Wadsworth, who sailed *Intrepid* on a fire-

Two fanciful representations of Stephen Decatur at Tripoli show the young lieutenant battling a fierce Barbary pirate, presumably the captain who killed his young brother. During the struggle, a wounded American sailor put his head (or, in some accounts, his arm) in the way of a scimitar stroke, thus saving Decatur's life. Tattoo mark in one picture wrongly attributes this deed to one Reuben James; in reality the sailor's name was Daniel Frazier. Two U.S. destroyers today are named the James and the Frazier. (Charles Phelps Cushing and U.S. Naval Academy from Cushing)

ship mission on September 4. The ketch had been stuffed with powder and combustibles attached to a fifteen-minute fuse; it was to be touched off as a huge floating bomb in the midst of the enemy fleet. Lieutenant Somers and his thirteen men never returned. A premature blast blew *Intrepid* to atoms before she ever reached the pirate ships. Lieutenant Wadsworth's memory would be perpetuated by his nephew and namesake, Henry Wadsworth Longfellow.

Preble returned home in modest triumph, to be commended by the President and to receive a gold medal from Congress — and to die of tuberculosis a year later. Pope Pius VII said that under Preble's orders Americans "had done more for the cause of Christianity than the most powerful nations of Christendom have done for ages."

Preble's successor, Captain Samuel Barron, was yet another senior naval officer handicapped by bad health. In those days few men who made the sea their life remained healthy; shipboard food was monotonous and bad, and diseases of all kinds took a heavy toll. Barron was fortunate to have as his second-in-command the vigorous John Rodgers, like Preble a fighting disciplinarian. The two men led the largest flotilla assembled under the American flag: six frigates, seven brigs, and ten gunboats whose trim appearance was much admired by the British naval critics at Gibraltar.

Aboard his flagship, Barron brought along an individual he looked upon with some disdain, William Eaton. The former consul had never been popular with the navy because of his outspoken opinion that most of its officers were too cautious, and that a "company of comedians" could maintain a blockade as well as Morris had done. Now, however, Eaton carried the odd title of Navy Agent to the Barbary States, and Barron was under discretionary orders to cooperate with him. William Eaton had persuaded the powers back in the new capital city of Washington that he knew how to end the long-drawn-out struggle with Tripoli.

Eaton's scheme, which was not especially original, called for no less than fomenting rebellion to supplant the pasha of Tripoli with his older brother, Hamet. Previously, Morris had dismissed the idea as insane, and Preble had been reluctant to try it for lack of support from his captains.

To achieve his grand design, the erstwhile army captain

A miniature of Lieutenant Presley N. O'Bannon, U.S. Marine Corps, who commanded the small Marine contingent on the march to Derna, Tripoli, in 1805. About thirty years old when he made the famous desert trek with "General" Eaton, O'Bannon was presented with a jeweled scimitar by the pasha for his gallantry. He retired from the Corps in 1807 and spent the remainder of his life in his native Kentucky. (U.S. Naval Academy Museum from Cushing)

had at his disposal $20,000 in cash, the little brig *Argus*, and a cadre of nine men. One of the latter was a midshipman with the memorable name of Pascal Paoli Peck, and the other eight were United States Marines led by Lieutenant Presley O'Bannon.

This handful of men would share in an incredible adventure, little recalled today except for a line in the *Marine Hymn*:

From the halls of Montezuma, to the shores of Tripoli.

The Almost Forgotten Hero

For a man who detested his job, William Eaton of Connecticut had kept busy as consul at Tunis. A speculator in shipping, he sent home olives, dates, and figs for experimental planting and acted as go-between for his fellow consuls Cathcart and O'Brien who hated each other. In the evenings he wandered about sketching the fortifications of Tunis, since he felt one never could tell when such intelligence might come in handy.

It had been Cathcart's idea, originally, to depose Yusuf as pasha of Tripoli in favor of his brother, Hamet. The latter was living in exile in Tunis largely at Eaton's expense. But Commodore Barron would have none of such skulduggery; in those days naval officers doubled in brass as agents of the State Department.

Now that Eaton had won approval for his scheme, he first had to find his puppet prince, for Hamet had forayed up the Nile to join in a rebellion against the Turks. The American brought his Tripolitan friend to Alexandria, where the two agreed to attack Yusuf's port of Derna. In that city Hamet had some support. To avoid an exhausting 500-mile march, Eaton wished to transport his Christian force by sea, but Hamet insisted that his own flighty followers might disappear into the desert if their leaders and American support did not march with them.

By promising riches after victory, "General" Eaton, as Hamet named him, had recruited probably the most hybrid "army" ever to have served the United States. The men were mostly Arabs and Levantines, with a sprinkling of Greeks and other European soldiers of fortune, and pickpockets. There were about six hundred in all. They were trailed by a train of camels, horses, drivers, women, and children. The mounts had been hired from desert sheiks with Eaton's own money, which he hoped later to regain from what otherwise would have to be paid as tribute by Sweden, Denmark, and Holland. Only he knew how such delicate financing was supposed to work.

The expedition would be supplied by sea, and *Argus*, Lieutenant Isaac Hull commanding, would pace the marchers just offshore. Hull was another of "Preble's Boys" about whom one day a song would be sung. Now he represented nearly all of Barron's naval support of Eaton. Moreover, it was Hull who provided the rabble army with its eight marines off the *Argus*.

The motley force moved out of Alexandria on March 8, 1805, along a route which was to be soaked in blood during World War II. Two of Eaton's halts were at Tobruk, later the scene of a long and desperate siege, and at El Alamein, where the decisive battle of that later war in North Africa would be fought. Like Eaton's army, those of the future would suffer under the sandstorms of the khamsin wind, bringing darkness

Hamet Bashaw and the American consul, "General" William Eaton (in cocked hat) on the march to Derna, Tripoli, 1805. At right, American Marines. (D.O.D., Marine Corps, from Cushing)

at midday, but in 1943 Marshals Montgomery and Rommel were spared having to handle the fickle soldiery with which Eaton had to contend.

For example, when his Arab cavalry threatened to mutiny, Eaton outfaced the boiling mob with a show of bayonets by his squad of marines. Eventually Eaton's personal fortune was

[43]

drained by his grand design; at times he had to borrow money from his marines and Greeks to pay his camel drivers.

As they neared Derna, Hamet's feet dragged, until suddenly he bolted, a victim of visions and uncertainty. His wife and children were being held hostage by Yusuf, who already had proven that brotherly love was not his outstanding virtue. Eaton had to search for and bring back his anxious pasha.

Lesser lights than Hamet also developed doubts about the wisdom of their mission. Eaton kept them in line by choking off their rations. When food ran low, everyone ate roots, fennel leaves, and at least one wildcat. When Arab women along the trail offered to sell them bunches of dates, Eaton discovered he could pay with buttons torn off European clothing. Once when their water ran out, he found a source which he kept secret — it was a well with two dead bodies in it.

The ingenious Yankee even invented a theology to smooth over relations with the Muslims. He told the Arabs that the United States was unique among the infidel nations, in that its heaven was quite separate from Europe's. In the afterlife, he assured them, Arab and American souls would be encouraged to go visiting in each other's paradise.

The *Argus* lost contact with the march about 90 miles from Derna, just as the land forces' food gave out. Some of the mercenaries now vowed to quit, but were coaxed into eating a pack camel and to wait a day or so. Fortunately the brig reappeared on April 16, followed by *Hornet* with food and munitions on the seventeenth. After a few days' rest, Eaton resumed his advance, arriving outside Derna on April 25.

To his demand for surrender, the Muslim defender replied stoutly, "My head or yours!" After two days of maneuvering, Eaton's lone cannon, backed by those of *Argus, Hornet,* and the messenger ship *Nautilus,* opened on Derna's stone walls and houses. The noise was impressive, the smell dusty, and in their excitement the Greek artillerymen burst their cannon by firing it with the rammer still in the tube. At four in the afternoon, Eaton ordered a frontal attack, and with his tiny force of eight American marines and fifty Greeks he charged the walls. Eaton and his men won the town at the relatively high cost of fourteen dead, two of them marines, and Eaton himself took a ball through the wrist. Midshipman George Mann, who had replaced P. P. Peck from the *Argus,* ran up the Stars and Stripes over the first city of the Old World captured by Americans.

The victors were besieged in Derna throughout the month of May, but Hamet's cavalry repulsed all attacks. Eaton begged Commodore Barron to proclaim Hamet the new pasha, but Barron declined to do this, having been quietly urging Consul Lear to come to terms with Yusuf. Barron also delayed reinforcing the army for a march on Tripoli, 700 miles to the west. What the fearless Eaton might have accomplished with a hundred or more of the marines who were idle aboard Barron's squadron is tantalizing to imagine.

On June 11, Eaton was thunderstruck by news that Tobias Lear had come to an agreement with Tripoli. To escape certain death at the hands of their angry followers, for whom the peace would end all prospects of loot, Eaton and Hamet fled. They, the marines, and the Christian mercenaries boarded

[45]

the U.S.S. *Constellation* secretly by night on June 13, thus ending the invasion of "the shores of Tripoli."

In November, Eaton was toasted at dinners given by the President and the Chief Justice of the United States, but Congress ignored him. It even delayed reimbursing him for money he had advanced, while his colleague Cathcart and others were promptly and amply rewarded. Even Eaton's adjutant, a villain answering variously to the names of Gervasio Santuari, Eugene Leitensdorfer, Carlo Hossondo, and Muart Aga, collected pay as "colonel of cavalry in Africa." Moreover, Leitensdorfer drew a mileage allowance for his march to Derna!

Rankling over what he thought was a sellout by Tobias Lear and a betrayal by Congress, Eaton denounced them to any and all who would listen. Eventually his accusations became so extreme that he made himself a public bore. In time, he received some compensation from Congress and a large tract of wild land in Maine. Aaron Burr offered this malcontented man a high place in the mysterious empire he would carve out of the west, but the basically loyal Eaton exposed Burr in court.

William Eaton died in 1811, a lonely drunkard who was scarcely missed — an almost forgotten hero.

The Almost Perfect Hero

Tobias Lear's treaty with the pasha of Tripoli called for the release of all prisoners, an end to slave-taking and ship seizure, and a final ransom payment of $60,000. Yusuf panted with eagerness to sign, but Lear may have been too hasty. Naval pressure was worrying the pirates, but even more they had been alarmed by the menace of William Eaton's ragtag army. Or so Eaton asserted as a mouthpiece for the Federalist opposition, loudly accusing President Jefferson of cowardice.

Captain John Rodgers with a few ships cowed the bey of Tunis in August, and that ruler sent a blooded horse as a gift to horseman Jefferson, who refused it. Thereafter, the blue Mediterranean became safe for American shipping for many months.

However, when Algiers detained three vessels in the fall of 1807, Lear bought freedom for $18,000. Modest as the sum was, it signaled the resumption of two bad habits, piracy and tribute. The renewal of these practices made a mockery of his principles as stated in the treaty with Tripoli.

The war with England during 1812–14 pushed the Bar-

[47]

bary pirates into a back closet of American concerns. In any event, retaliation against the corsairs would have been impossible, for after 1812 the navy of the United States was swept from the seas by the British. That "huge, shaggy beast," the dey of Algiers, took advantage of Consul Lear's helplessness by picking his pocket of $11,000 before expelling him in July, 1812. The American had to borrow the money to escape being worked in chains, as had the Danish consul not long before.

Not long after this, the dey announced a "policy to increase the number of my American slaves," whereupon he captured the brig *Edwin* and its crew in August. This dey was the fifth of his royal line to seize American ships; all of his predecessors had been assassinated, and none recognized the agreements made by those who had gone before him. President James Madison bided his time until he could settle the chronic Algerian nuisance forever.

On March 2, 1815, ten weeks after the end of her war with England, the United States formally declared war on Algiers. The President dispatched retribution, long delayed but richly deserved, in the form of ten tall ships under the command of Stephen Decatur. Another squadron under the command of William Bainbridge was organized to follow, but with Bainbridge's usual luck, by the time he arrived in the Mediterranean the show was over.

Decatur and His Expedition

In some quarters today it is fashionable to disparage men of simple faith like Stephen Decatur. He is often remembered merely as a patriot because of the words usually misquoted as "My country, right or wrong." There was much more to Decatur than that.

As a leader he was generous with praise when it was earned, and more remarkably he was kind to his men in a day when sailors were flogged as readily as fed. A marine wrote of him that "not a tar, who ever sailed with Decatur, but would almost sacrifice his life for him."

Moreover, Decatur was a skilled naval administrator as well as a faultless tactician. He was also an inventor, a marine zoologist, a linguist, a student of history, and a lover of poetry, music, and art. These talents, combined with cheerfulness, wit, good looks, an athletic body, and unflinching courage, make him an almost perfect hero for all seasons.

The punitive expedition which Decatur led arrived off Algiers in June. He promptly shot up the flagship of the dey's fleet, capturing it with 486 prisoners. Decatur then sent a blunt

A painting showing the bombardment of Algiers in 1816. (Charles Phelps Cushing)

ultimatum to the dey: Free every slave at once, pay an indemnity of $10,000 to the survivors of the brig *Edwin*, and cease all demands for tribute forever. Decatur indicated that he would stand for no nonsense; the longer consent was delayed, the more Algerian ships he would sink.

Numbed by shock, the dey whined that perhaps there had been a "misunderstanding" which he would like to correct for "the amiable James Madison, the Emperor of America." Although drawn in 1816, the treaty wrung from Algiers was not ratified for six years, but by no fault of Congress. Incredibly, someone in the State Department mislaid it for all that time.

The bey of Tunis groomed his beard with a diamond-encrusted comb as he complained, "Why do they send wild young men to treat for peace with the old powers?" Still, he paid Decatur $46,000 to go away. In its turn, Tripoli felt the hand of the relentless Decatur, paying him a $25,000 indemnity and freeing its slaves, including some bewildered but very happy Danes and Italians.

The "old powers" never again molested any American ships. Decatur's swift and firm action impelled England to follow the American example a year later; the "degrading yoke" of tribute she had permitted for more than one hundred and fifty years was being lifted.

A tactless jibe by the dey of Algiers may have spurred England's decision. His Highness had taunted the British consul about Decatur's flagship *Guerrière*, named for a British frigate that had been pounded to kindling by *Constitution* in 1812. Also in the American squadron had been *Macedonian*, captured in battle in 1812 by *United States*, Captain Stephen Decatur commanding.

The dashing captain returned to the United States to be lionized by a grateful nation. Among the honors accorded him were parades, songs, dinners, a dress sword from Congress, and a public commendation by the President. Decatur became somewhat embarrassed by it all. One day at Norfolk, Virginia, he responded to a round of patriotic toasts; a newspaper reported that what he said was, "Our country! In her intercourse with foreign nations may she always be in the right; but our country, right or wrong."

Yet Stephen Decatur died a senseless death on March 22, 1820, after a pistol duel with James Barron. Bad blood had festered between the two men; Decatur had been assigned to investigate Captain Barron's surrender of *Chesapeake* to British *Leopard* in 1807 after only a token resistance. Decatur's report criticizing Barron for an unready ship had resulted in censure and suspension for Barron.

But that had been thirteen years before they fought a duel neither wanted. Indeed, Barron called dueling "a barbarous practice," and there is some belief that he was a pawn maneuvered to fight by other men jealous of the almost perfect hero.

Stephen Decatur's last words were in keeping with his entire life. His only sorrow, he said, was that he had not died in the service of his country.

The Significance of the Barbary Wars

Certain results of the Barbary expeditions stand out clearly, such as the suppression of piracy, the beginning of a U.S. Navy and Marine Corps with their proud traditions, and the proof that acting together as a nation was no threat to states' rights.

Yet beyond these results the Tripolitan War produced something unique: the American as an American had made his presence known in a world of old empires.

For the first time, the new nation recognized its own authentic heroes. For unlike their Revolutionary fathers of 1776, the young men who fought the corsairs of Barbary had never known what it was to serve any other nation than the United States of America.

What John Quincy Adams said of Stephen Decatur might well apply to each. The United States had produced "one who has illustrated its history and given grace and dignity to its character in the eyes of the world."

[53]

Appendix

The American naval officers who served during the Barbary wars were apprentices who flowered brilliantly in the unwanted war against England in 1812. For a brief moment their victories astonished the world, until one by one they were captured or bottled up in harbor. England's sea power, though deeply committed to the struggle against Napoleon, still vastly overmatched anything the United States had. The British could send 37 frigates against each and every one of the 8 flying the American flag. And in ships of the line, the big 74-gun three-deckers, the count was 219 to none.

Nevertheless "Preble's Boys" did their old master proud. Among the most noteworthy of them were these:

William Bainbridge (1774–1833) — captain of *Constitution* when she destroyed *Java* in two hours, 1812.

James Biddle (1783–1848) — captain of the brig *Hornet* which took *Penguin* in twenty-two minutes, 1815.

William Burrows (1785–1813) — captain of *Enterprise* which captured *Boxer* in forty minutes; he and his British opponent were killed and are buried together at Portland, Maine.

Stephen Decatur (1779–1820) — as captain of *United States*, which he had helped to build, took *Macedonian* as prize, 1812.

Isaac Hull (1773–1843) — captain of *Constitution* in her most famous battle, when *Guerrière* was reduced to burning splinters in thirty minutes, 1812.

Jacob Jones (1768–1850) — captain of the sloop *Wasp* which took *Frolic* in forty-three minutes, 1812.

James Lawrence (1781–1813) — captain of the brig *Hornet* which sank *Peacock* in eleven minutes. He died four months later aboard *Chesapeake* in defeat by *Shannon*, calling, "Don't give up the ship!"

Thomas MacDonough (1783–1825) — commander on Lake Champlain, who built a fleet and defeated an invasion from Canada, 1814.

Oliver Hazard Perry (1785–1819) — as commander on Lake Erie, defeated British fleet, 1813, and reported, "We have met the enemy and they are ours."

David Porter (1780–1843) — captain of *Essex* which took first capture of the war, the sloop *Alert*, in five minutes, 1812.

John Rodgers (1773–1838) — commanded the Atlantic squadron, 1812; first of an unbroken line of naval officers of his name, till the death of the last in a plane crash, 1926.

Charles Stewart (1778–1869) — as captain of *Constitution* in her last fight, captured *Cyane* and *Levant*, 1815, two months after peace.

Selected Bibliography

Allen, G. W. *Our Naval War with France*

————. *Our Navy and the Barbary Corsairs*

Donovan, Frank. *The Tall Frigates*

Encyclopedia Americana

Irwin, R.W. *Diplomatic Relations of the United States with the Barbary Powers*

Knox, D. W. *The United States Navy*

Lewis, C. L. *The Romantic Decatur*

Morison, S. E. *The Oxford History of the American People*

Paullin, C. O. *Diplomatic Negotiations of American Naval Officers*

Tucker, Glenn. *Dawn Like Thunder*

Wright, L. B. & Macleod, J. H. *The First Americans in North Africa*

Index

[61]

[62]